Country Dezeebob

Alien I

Jokes and Cartoons
Over 170 Pages and 350 Illustrations

Desi Northup
The Cartoon Guru

Made in the USA

Published in the United States by Desno Publishing Co. All rights reserved. No part of this book may be reproduced in any manner whatsoever without written permission from the publisher, except in the case of brief quotations from articles and reviews. Artwork is, also, not to be duplicated or reproduced.

Desno Publishing Co.
Route 3 Hopkinton NH 03229
Copyright 2014 Desi Northup

What did the alien say to the messy garden?

Take me to your weeder.

What do you say when you greet an alien with four heads?

Hello, hello, hello, hello.

Mother alien: "Don't eat with your fingers.

Use a shovel like I taught you."

Did you hear about the space monster who thought he had bad eyesight?

He discovered it was all right when he got his hair cut.

What's the difference between a space monster with fleas and a bored guest?

One's going to itch and the other is itching to go.

Which space monster is making strange noises in its throat?

A gargoyle.

What's the best way to avoid infection from biting space monsters?

Don't bite any.

What happened to Ray when he met a space monster?

He became X-Ray.

Why did the space monster sit on a bag of tomatoes?

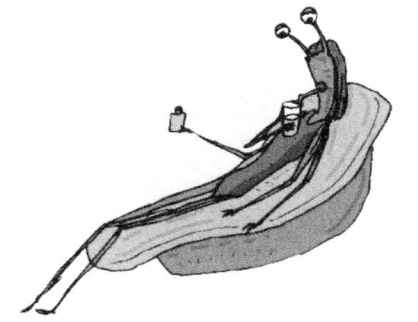

Because she wanted to play squash.

What do you call a robot who always goes the longest way round on a journey?

R2 Detour.

Where was the alien when the lights went out in his ship?

In the dark.

Why did the Martian go to the optician?

He had stars in his eyes.

What's round, purple and spines through the space?

The planet of the Grapes.

Why won't world never come to an end?

Because its round.

Why was the alien called Wonder Boy at school?

Because everyone used to look at him and wonder.

What's wooly, covered in chocolate and travels around the sun?

A Mars bar.

"That alien has pedestrian eyes."
"What do you mean?"

"They look both ways before they cross."

Where are all aliens beautiful?

They're in the dark.

Why did the alien take a bath?

So he could make a clean getaway.

Did you hear about the alien who sent his photo to a Lonely Hearts Club?

They sent it back saying they weren't that lonely.

Did you hear about the alien who rode a tricycle that went around biting people?

It was known as the vicious cycle.

Why did the alien wear a bullet-proof vest?

Because of all the shooting stars.

"We can probably make Mars in one day."

"That spacesuit fits you like a bandage."

"Yes, I got it by accident."

Why did the alien girl walk sideways?

Her boyfriend told her she had a beautiful profile.

How can an alien stop a cold in his head from going to his chest?

Tie a knot in his neck.

Why don't astronauts keep their jobs for very long?

Because as soon as they start, they are fired.

How does an alien intruder get into your house?

Intruder door.

Did you hear about the alien who went to a mind reader and paid to have his thoughts read?

She gave him his money back.

Why was the robot silly?

He had a screw loose.

Why do bald aliens never use keys?

Because they haven't any locks.

Why did the alien scratch herself?

Because no one else knew where she itched.

Where are aliens found?

"We don't visit this branch often enough."

They are so clever they are never lost.

What do you get if you cross a spaceship computer with an elastic band?

A computer that makes snap decisions.

~ 19 ~

How did the young alien get his hands so dirty? He washed his face with them.

When a window is like a star?

When it's a skylight.

What belongs to an alien but it's used more by others?

His name.

Why did the robot take his nose apart?

To see how it ran.

How does an alien shave?

With a laser blade.

What do you get if you cross an alien with an owl?

Someone that scares everyone but doesn't give a hoot.

"Thanks for the chow ... any chance you could toss up my lead boots?"

Why did the robot cross the road?

Because he was following the chicken.

~ 23 ~

Why are mad aliens like biscuits?

Because they are crackers.

Why do aliens wear dark glasses?

So no one can recognize them.

What do you get if you cross an alien with a fridge?

I don't know, but when you take its helmet off you can't see for the light shining in your eyes.

Why did the one-eyed aliens always fight?

They could never see eye to eye about anything.

~ 25 ~

Why did the robot yawn?

He was suffering from metal fatigue.

Why did the robot stop smoking?

He had his fuse box repaired.

What goes "ha, ha, crash"?

A robot laughing her head off.

Who won the alien's beauty contest?

Nobody.

Why did the robot eat little bits of metal all day?

It was his staple diet.

What kind of alien has the best hearing?

The eariest.

What's a giant alien's favorite story?

A tall tale.

How can you tell if a robot's been in your fridge?

By the little bits of metal in your butter.

Why did the alien think there was something wrong with her finger?

Every time she put it in her nose, she went deaf.

Why are talking heads always lonely?

Because they have no body.

"I just invented a mechanical frog."
"What does it say?"

"It goes robot, robot, robot."

What do the Martians like to watch on TV every-year?

The Out-of-this-World Series.

Why did the Neptunian cross the road?

It didn't want to be mistaken for a chicken.

Why couldn't the Blob land on the moon?

It was already full.

What do you get if you cross a Venusian with a skunk?

Something that stinks to high heaven.

A Martian landed on a beach near Miami and took out his skies. One of the beachgoers stared at him.

Earthling: "What are you doing with those skis? You are on Miami Beach. There is never any snow here."

Martian: "That's OK. It's coming with the rest of my luggage."

How do you measure eyeballs? In inches. They don't have feet.

How do Martians serve dinner in outer space?

On flying saucers.

Where should 300-pound Martian go?

On a diet.

What's the difference between
a Martian and a doughnut?

You can't dunk a Martian
in your coffee.

What looks just like a half of
a Martian?

The other half.

Why did the alien think grass was dangerous?

He heard it was full of blades.

What game do astronauts like to play better than any other?

Moon-opoly.

Why does E.T. have such big eyes?

He saw his phone bill.

Two robots on Mars were talking.
"I'll love you forever," the boy robot said, "or for 250,000 miles.

Whichever comes first."

What do astronauts do at Christmas time?

They kiss under the missile-toe.

What do you call an alien spaceship that drips water?

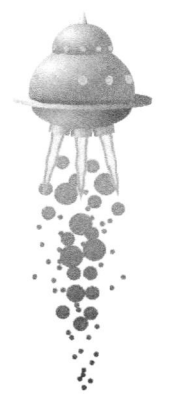

A crying saucer.

Why do Martians suspect that walls keep secrets?

Because they are always meeting in the corner.

A Martian and his girlfriend were looking at the objects inside the window at the hardware store. "You see that toaster and the microwave oven?" The Martian said. "They are on sale. Why don't you buy them?"

"No," his girlfriend replied. "I don't look good in a bikini."

Two earthlings getting into a rocket ship: "Tell the control tower we don't want to go faster than sound because we want to talk to each other on the trip."

Why are robots so brave?

They have nerves of steel.

What do you get if you cross a baby with an alien spaceship?

An unidentified crying object.

What do you call a fat alien?

An extra cholesterol.

How do aliens shave in the morning?

With a laser blade.

Why was the alien happy when it came back from the tailors?

His trousers fitted him like a glove.

What robot knows the quickest way to any star system?

X-14 detour.

Why was the alien green?

It hadn't taken
its space sickness pills.

Do robots have brothers?

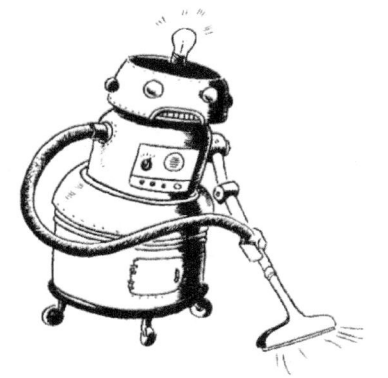

No, but they do have tran-sisters.

What should you do if a huge seven eyed alien rolls its eyes at you?

Roll them back – quick.

How can you tell if the moon is happy?

See if it's beaming.

Which planet in the solar system did the alien crash land on?

Splaturn.

What happened to the silly alien that wondered where our sun had gone?

By the next morning it had dawned on him.

When does the moon stop eating?

When it's full.

How do planets greet each other?

Pleased to meteor.

What happened when Ray discovered an alien with a laser gun?

He became an ex-Ray.

What did the mother star say to the child star?

You shouldn't be out at night.

What did the alien do with the arms that fell off when he grew new ones?

He kept them. He thought they might come in handy.

~ 51 ~

What did the boy say when the teacher asked which was nearer - India or the Moon? The moon, because you never see India, but you can see the moon at night.

Where should a 500 pound alien go?

On a diet.

Why should you never go to the movies on the moon?

It lacks atmosphere.

How do you help a baby astronaut to sleep?

You rock-et.

What's the daftest thing you can see at night?

A fool moon.

What is a space alien's favorite thing to have on toast?

Baked beings.

"You have no idea what a guy will do to get out of rush hour traffic."

What did the boy say when the teacher asked – what do you see at planetariums?

Starfish.

What kind of alien spaceship gets upset easily?

A crying saucer.

What's the best way to talk to aliens?

From a long way away.

What kind of star always ends up in jail?

A shooting star.

What would you get if you crossed a UFO with a wizard?

A flying sorcerer.

Which of the Star Wars characters gradually disappeared?

Darth Fader.

How would throwing eggs at aliens destroy them?

They'd be eggs-terminated.

Which of the Star Wars characters liked to wander up to his thighs in rivers?

Darth Wader.

What steps should you take if you see an alien?

Large ones.

What did the Emperor say when asked to pay the waitress for lunch?

Darth Paid-her.

What is an alien's favorite soup?

Scream of tomato.

When is it difficult to get on the moon?

When it is full.

How do aliens like their cups of tea?

On flying saucers.

What's the difference between an alien and a cookie?

Have you ever tried dunking an alien in your milk?

What drink don't spacemen have in outer space?

Gravi-tea.

Why do scientists believe there is life on Mars?

Someone stole the wheels off the Mars Rover.

What's the difference between an alien and potatoes?

You should never try mashing an alien.

Where do aliens go for their holidays?

Earth – for their annual trip around the Sun.

What's got two tentacles, a huge head and wants you to shock it?

An alien with hiccups.

Why did the sun go to school and then college?

It wanted to be brighter.

Why are aliens forgetful?

Everything goes in one ear and out the others.

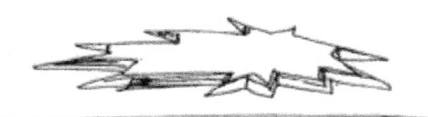

"I'll take you to my leader ... right after I take you to my insurance agent."

What kind of mad insect lives on the moon?

A luna-tic.

What is the difference between an invading alien fleet and a candy bar?

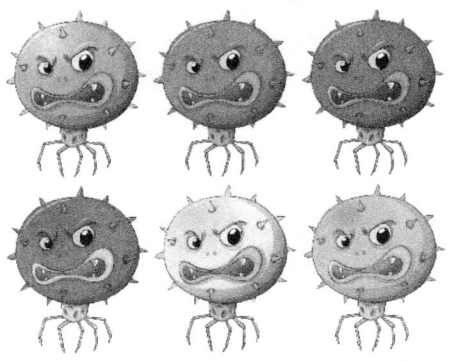

People like candy.

What is the cow's favorite object in space? The Mooooon.

What can aliens do that humans can't?

Count to 50 on their fingers.

What else can aliens do that humans can't?

Count to 100 on their toes.

What do astronauts read to enjoy themselves?

Comet books.

When do aliens eat fluorescent lamps?

Whenever they need light refreshments.

What does an alien press on a keyboard to launch a saucer?

The spacebar.

What was Mickey Mouse doing on Neptune?

Looking for Pluto.

Why did the alien cross the road?

It wanted to learn more about the lives of chickens.

What do you do if you find a space man?

Park in it... man.

What do you give an alien with six huge feet?

Three pairs of flippers.

Why are astronauts careful when cooking meals?

In case they see an unidentified frying object.

How do you get ten aliens in a pickle jar?

Eat the pickles first.

Why is it difficult to keep your job if you're an astronaut?

They are always getting fired.

What happened when the police tried to find an alien with one eye? They had more luck when they started using both eyes.

How do we know astronauts are angry all the time?

They are always blasting off.

"As a member of the worldwide web,
I would like to officially welcome you to Earth."

What do you get if you cross a student and an alien?

Something from another universe -ity.

Why did the space alien become known as Captain Kirk?

It had a left ear, a right ear and a final front ear.

Why are spacemen so successful?

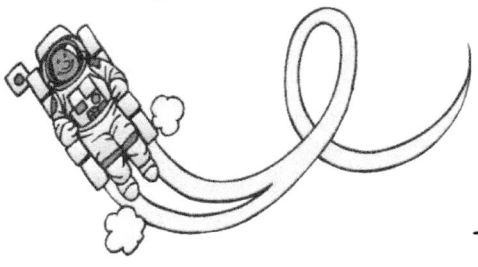

They are always going up in the world.

Where do the scariest of all space aliens live?

In a far distant terror-tory.

How do galaxies hold up their trousers?

With asteroid belts.

What happened when the boy announced he could lift an alien with both hands tied?

He couldn't find an alien that was tied up.

What do cartoon characters living on the moon enjoy listening to?

Luna Tunes.

Why do barbers never cut the hair of aliens with ray guns?

It's easier with scissors.

What lights spin around the Earth?

Satel-lites.

What happens if you upset a man-eating alien?

You end up in hot water.

What are the planet's favorite songs?

Nep-tunes.

How do cows move about the galaxy?

Through the Milky Way.

What meteorites get their sums wrong at school?

Meteo-wrongs.

What did Jupiter say to Saturn at the end of the phone call?

Give me a ring.

How does the moon get its hair cut?

Eclipse it.

What happened to the alien who crossed a toad with the sun?

He got star warts.

"Our only hope is to pick its wings off. That's why I brought Arnold in."

Why don't aliens eat in restaurants?

Once they've eaten the waiter there is no-one left to bring their main meal.

Where did the aliens leave their UFOs?

At parking meteors.

What game should you never play with 10 feet tall aliens?

Squash.

What did the alien that wanted a bedtime story say?

Take me to your reader.

How do aliens like to cook humans?

Terror-fried.

What did the hungry alien say?

Take me to your feeder.

What did the alien wear in summer?

Three pairs of sunglasses - one for each head.

What did the super-fast alien say?

Take me to your speeder.

What happens if a two ton alien eats your piano?

You get flat notes.

What's the best thing to become if you've got high hopes?

A spaceman.

What happens if you train a two ton alien to walk on a lead?

You'll need to scoop some big poops.

What do alien's love to play at parties?

Hide-and-go-shriek.

What is an alien's favorite cheese?

Scream cheese.

What's huge with ten arms, twelve legs and goes… Beep. Beep.?

An alien in a traffic jam.

Why did the crazy space alien eat a couch and three chairs?

It had a suite tooth.

What are crazy spacemen called?

Astronuts.

How did a hideous alien persuade a pretty girl to kiss it?

With a stun gun.

At this point, the theory that people in chicken suits were immune to the death ray was unproven.

What's green with five eyes and goes up and down, up and down?

An alien stuck in a tractor beam.

When do astronauts eat?

At launch time.

Why do aliens wear helmets?

So they don't scare themselves when they look in the mirror.

What do lady aliens with huge teeth do at human parties?

They look for edible bachelors.

What was Captain Kirk doing when he went into the ladies bathroom?

Boldly going where no man has been before.

What did the man say to the huge alien that wanted to be a train driver?

I won't stand in your way.

What game do aliens play?

Astronauts and crosses.

How can you tell if you've met a good alien?

You can talk about it later.

What kind of alien spaceship gets upset easily?

A crying saucer.

How do you help a baby alien to sleep?

You rock-et.

What did the alien do with the arms that fell off when he grew new ones?

He kept them –
he said they might come in handy.

What would you call an alien who was born on Mars, lived on Venus and died on Saturn?

Dead.

Why did the alien put a mouse in his space rocket?

He wanted to make a little go a long way.

What did planet Earth say to planet Saturn?

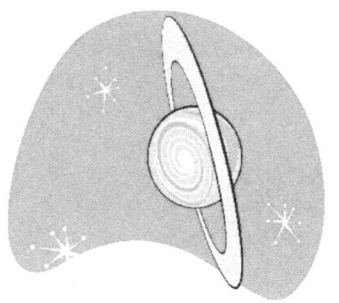

"You must give me a ring sometime."

Which is the moon monster's least favorite day?

Sunday.

What do you call a space kangaroo?

An Austr-alien.

Which side of a spaceship is the safest to sit in?

The inside.

"I'll take you to my leader ... right after I take you to my insurance agent."

Why don't space scientists like to study moon rocks?

Because that's a very hard subject.

What do you call empty spacesuits?

Astro-noughts.

What did the astronaut say to the invisible space monster?

"I haven't seen very much of you lately."

What game do space monsters play when it rains?

Moon-opoly.

What did the alien say to the chicken?

Eggs-terminate.

What do space monsters have on their toast?

Mars-malade.

Where do space priests live?

In a moon-astery.

What do alien boy scouts sing?

"Tin can, gooley gooley gooley..."

What did a space monster say when it saw a rocket landing?

"Oh good, tinned food."

One Alien: "I hear you visited the Paper Planet. How was it?"

Second Alien: "Tear-able."

"Doctor, Doctor! I keep thinking I'm a Martian!"

"Don't be silly. You are not from Mars, you from Venus, just like me."

Why did the alien keep metal polish in her rocket?

She wanted to rise and shine.

How does a robot dog eat his food?

He just woofs it down.

Did you hear about the robot with a half dozen arms?

She was handy to have around.

What do you call an alien magician?

A flying sorcerer.

"Doctor, Doctor! I keep thinking I'm the moon."

"What's come over you?"
"Several cows
and a cat with a fiddle."

Why did the alien step on a chocolate bar?

He wanted to set foot on Mars.

What is the alien's favorite soft drink?

Lemon and slime.

What is the most musical planet in the solar system?

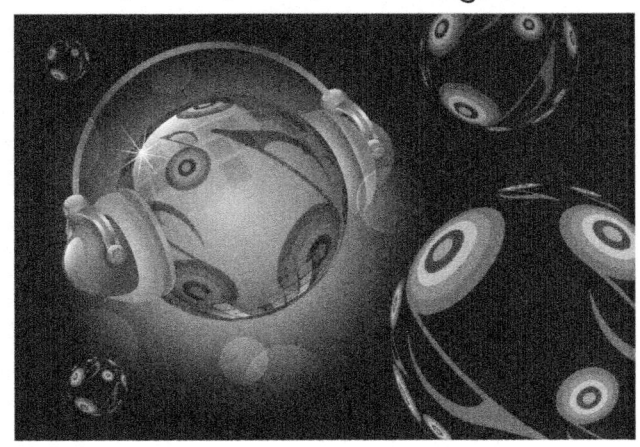

Nep-tune.

"See what happens when you reach for a cookie?"

Why is it easy to fool a space monster?

Because he has many legs to pull.

Why did the alien paint his spaceship bright red?

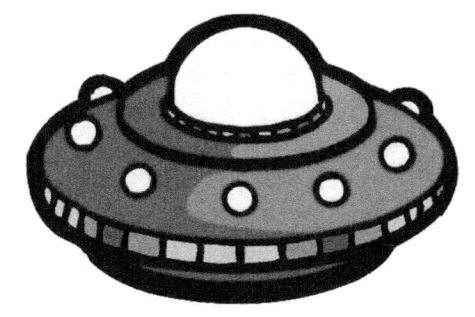

He wanted a tomato saucer.

Why did the alien want a tomato saucer?

So no other ship could ketchup with it.

What's green and slimy and tells stories with happy endings?

A fairy t-alien.

What did Captain Kirk say when he wanted a pet dog?

"Beam me up a Scottie."

What's smelly, has pointed ears and lives on the Starship Enterprise?

Mr. Sock.

Why did the space monster have green spots all over her body?

Because if she had purple ones she'd look silly.

Who swings on through outer space on a creeper?

Starzan.

What do you call someone who's crazy about aliens?

An Astro-nut.

Why did the alien army send their soldiers to Mars?

So they could spend the whole day Martian up and down.

What happened to the robot with a sore throat?

It had to have
 its tin-sels out.

How do aliens go fishing?

With a plan-net.

What kind of fish do they try to catch?

Starfish.

What is the worst bait to use for starfish?

Earth worms.

What do you call a mummy in a rocket?

Tutankha-moon.

How do aliens play badminton?

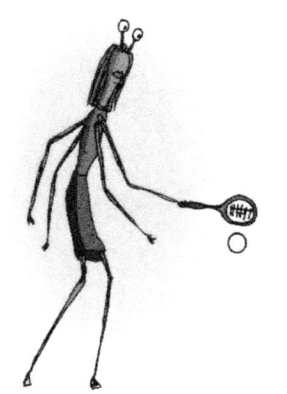

With a space shuttle.

"Why did I move to the moon? It's an interesting story."

When are moon monsters most scary?

When there is an eek-lipse.

Why did the alien policemen say, "Stop right there, stop right there, stop right there" to the alien?

Because it had three heads.

How many aliens does it take to launch a rocket?

5...4...3...2...1.

Why did the alien leave his wristwatch in his rocket?

He wanted to make time fly.

Do robots like to eat raisins?

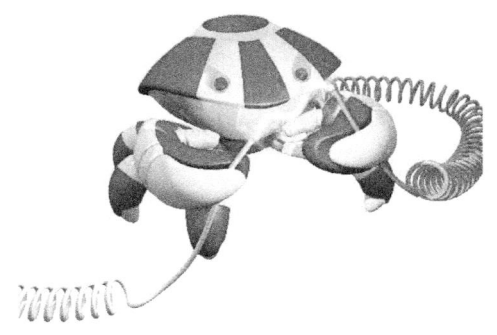

No, but they are very fond of electric currants.

Which planet has the hungriest aliens?

Chew-piter.

What do you call a broken spaceship?

An Unidentified Flying Reject.

What should you sing to an alien who's just arrived on this planet?

"Happy Earth-day to you!"

What's E.T's favorite TV show?

"Phone Home and Away".

Did you hear about short-sighted alien?

She went for an eye, eye, eye, eye, eye test.

Where do the smelliest aliens live?

Somewhere in the garlic-sy.

What spaceships do smelly aliens drive?

Phew. F.O.s

An alien had fifteen hands— which one did he use to stir his spaceship?

He didn't, he used the wheel.

What's the moon monster's favorite shampoo?

Wash and glow.

Robot 1: "Can you tell me if the bulb on top of my head is working?"

Robot 2: "Yes, no, yes, no, yes, no, yes, no, yes, no..."

Why did the alien pupil bring an apple to school?

Because he wanted to be creature's pet.

What flowers grow on the other side of the moon?

Sun flowers.

"Boo! I'm a space monster".

"You certainly are ----
you've got a lot of space
between your ears".

What did one space rock say to the other space rock?

"Meteor at the corner?"

What is the last thing an alien does before he goes to sleep?

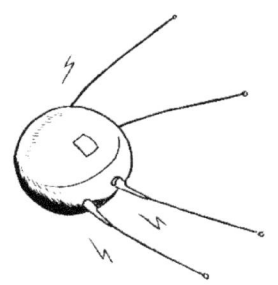

He switches off the satel-lite.

What do you call an alien in Santa Clause suit?

A U.F.Hohoho.

What do you call an alien nursery rhyme?

A uni-verse.

Why is it expensive to holiday among the stars?

Because the prices are astronomical.

What is an alien's favorite part of the news paper?

The star signs.

Why should you keep an eye on a sick alien?

In case he takes Saturn for the worse.

Why was an alien playing football in his flying saucer?

He was practicing for the cup.

What do you call an elderly Martian?

A grey-lien.

Why did the alien's rocket factory close down?

He couldn't get his business of the ground.

Where do you go to see Venusian cows?

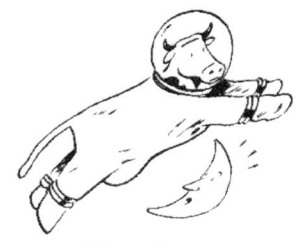

A science fiction moo-vie.

Why did the alien have a frog in his spaceship?

He only wanted to go on a short hop.

Why didn't the space monster need a musical instrument?

She already had her own horns.

Why did the alien put a laundry machine in his spaceship?

He wanted to go for a spin.

Which part of an alien's foot was shaped like a planet?

His Plu-toe.

Have you heard about the new alien diet?

They only eat Earthlings who are under 300 calories.

Why was there an alien spaceship in the bathroom?

Because someone left the landing light on.

Which is the world's largest see?

The galax-sea.

What do you call two aliens having a fight?

Science friction.

What did the giant alien say to the midget alien?

"Let's play squash."

Why do multi-eyed aliens make good teachers?

They're used to controlling lots of pupils.

Why did the alien fill his spaceship with jelly and custard?

He wanted to make it go a trifle faster.

Have you heard the joke about the time machine?

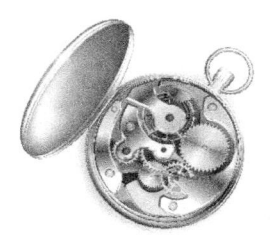

No. But someone is going to tell me tomorrow.

Why did the alien buy bird seed?

He wanted to grow some birds.

What's grey, craggy and zooms around the Mediterranean Sea?

The Rocket of Gibraltar.

What's white and fluffy and full of aliens?

A Mars-mallow.

What did the triangular alien say to the square alien?

"I haven't seen you around for ages."

Where would you catch the space train?

At the space station.

Why didn't the six-armed alien need gas put in his spaceship?

Three aliens create enough gas.

Why was the alien crossing his legs?

He was dying to make a pit stop.

Where do aliens go for their beverages?

Spaceola Store.

Why did the alien wear blue trousers?

They matched his blue top.

Why did the alien climbed into his spaceships gas tank?

He liked making a fuel of himself.

What is an alien's favorite subject at school?

Arts and spacecrafts.

What do you call an alien with four eyes?

An aliiiien.

What do aliens put on their Christmas cake?

Star-zipan.

Why didn't the left-handed alien appear in the space movie?

He wasn't right for the part.

What do you call a group of alien babies?

Star Trek-the knicks generation.

Why did the alien fill his spaceship with metal fasteners?

He wanted to give it a bit more zip.

Why did the aliens have Planet Earth painted on their glasses?

Because she wanted to see the world.

What's the quickest way to spot an alien?

Give it chicken pox.

What is the astronaut's motto?

"If at first you don't succeed,
fly, fly again."

Why did the kangaroo carry
an alien in her pouch?

Because
she was a Mars-upial.

Why did the robot have a light on top of his head?

Just in case he had any bright ideas.

What's the most boring science fiction movie?

Snore Wars.

What's nasty, breaths heavily and shouts "One hundred and eighty"?

Darts Vader.

What's grey, has a hole in the middle and flies to the moon?

An Apollo mint.

Why do space monsters have bad breath?

It takes a long time to brush 1,578,246 teeth.

Why don't space monsters know they have bad breath?

Would you tell someone who had 1,578,246 teeth?

When do aliens get their feet stuck together?

Once in a glue moon.

What do you say to a smelly alien on her birthday?

"For cheese a jolly good fellow."

What did one moon monster say to the other moon monster?

"Here we glow, here we glow, here we glow!"

What do you call an alien with feet shaped like stars?

Twinkle toes.

How do moon monsters watch Earth TV?

Through their telly-scopes.

What's the spiciest planet in the solar system?

Mer-curry.

Why do donkeys know a lot about aliens?

Because they are good at ass-tronomy.

Why should you never let aliens from Saturn use your bath?

They might leave rings.

Why did the alien have a dog in his spaceship?

He wanted to go pup, pup and away.

What's the slowest thing in the galaxy?

A snail-ien.

What did the robot say to the gas pump?

"Take your finger out of your ear when I'm talking to you."

What do you call a clumsy space explorer?

A disastronaut.

What did the robot have for a snack?

Fish and computer chips.

What do you call a robot that eats lots of chips?

Heavy metal.

What has two arms and one wheel?

A robot on a uni-cycle.

Passenger alien: "Is this bus running on time?"

Driver alien:
   "No, it's running on gas."

Why did the alien waitress put a spaceship I her dishwasher?

She wanted to take it for a spin.

Why didn't the alien music teacher need an instrument?

She already had her own horn.

Why did the alien put a frog in his pants?

He wanted to go for a short hop.

"Where would you find Martian cows?"

"In a science fiction movie."

Why was the alien playing football in his flying saucer?

He was practicing to win the cup.

Why is it expensive to go to space school?

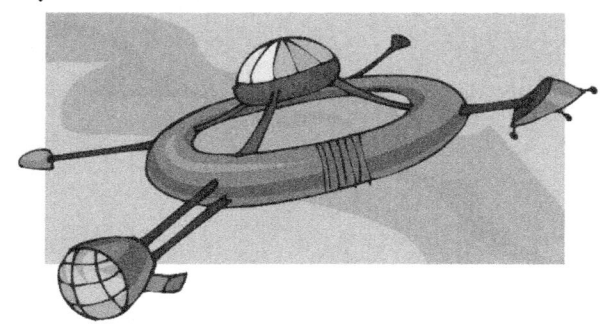

Because the fees are astronomical.

Alien teacher: "Shall I read you War of the Worlds?"
Pupil: "Is that the novel where Earth is saved from an invasion?"
Alien teacher: "That's right."

Pupil: "No thanks, I prefer the stories with happy endings."

"I hear our new teacher is one The Stone's, men from Saturn."

"Yes and all he ever plays is rock."

Why should a sick alien be kept home from school?

In case he takes Saturn for the worse.

"I appreciate the concept of universal health care, but there are limits."

"What did our new teach do before he became a teacher?"

"He ran a rocket factory, but it closed down."

"Why did it do that?"

"He could never get his business off the ground.

"My cell phone's not getting reception, mind if I use the phone booth?"

What is the alien teacher's favorite part of the newspaper?

The star signs.

What does Father Christmas say when he visits aliens?

U.F.Hohoho.

This book *is another publication in the **Chromicals™** series; a trademark of Desno Publishing Co.*

Chromicals ™

Description of an object, word, phrase or event presented and displayed in a manner with continually changing font sizes and styles, accompanied by an illustration that further defines the description of that subject, generally with a degree of comic relief.

You caN FiNd tHeSe aNd MaNy otHer BOOKS by DESI NORTHUP either ON-LiNe or at a BookStore Near you.

Desi Northup
The Cartoon Guru

Country Dezeebob

Printed in Great Britain
by Amazon